FAN GEYSER, FIRE-HOLE BASIN.

D0032890

The Yellowstone National Park

by John Muir

EDITOR'S PREFACE

"The Yellowstone National Park" was penned by John Muir, the explorer-naturalist, in 1898. It was then published as an article in *Atlantic* Monthly and again in 1901 as a chapter in Muir's book *Our National Parks*, and may well be his most literary piece of nature writing. At least it does contain his most-often quoted expression:

Climb the mountains and get their good tidings. Nature's peace will flow into you as sunshine flows into trees. The winds will blow their own freshness into you, and the storms their energy, while cares will drop off like autumn leaves.

Californians naturally claim Muir, as that state was his adopted home, and so it will likely come as a surprise—even a shock and disappointment—to many persons that this quotation was inspired by the Yellowstone of the Rocky Mountains rather than the Yosemite of the Sierra Nevada. But there are many more equally meaningful passages in this material. Yellowstone must have inspired him indeed!

In a way it was unfortunate that this article on Yellowstone fell into Muir's work on the national parks, for somehow that book has dropped into relative obscurity. Perhaps the book became dated as new national parks were established, carrying the seeds of its own destruction. This reprint changes that, making the writing available again to a broad audience. To make the material more appealing to today's readers, illustrations from sources contemporary to the late 1800s have been added: these include *Rambles in Wonderland* (1878), *Wonders of the Yellowstone* (1873), *America Illustrated* (1883), *Picturesque California* (1888), and *The Memorial Story of America* (1892).

Writing about the national parks in 1901 was easier than now. There were only four parks then—Yosemite, Sequoia, General Grant (now part of Kings Canyon), and Yellowstone. Yet Muir's work did not stop with the four extant parks. As he had had a hand in establishing three of these parks (all but Yellowstone), he went on in other chapters of *Our National Parks* to survey the entire nation, outlining America's natural features and their conservation needs and recommending more preserves. Partly as a result, although there have been many other influences as well, today there are more than 50 national parks and a total of some 380 units in the National Park System.

At Yellowstone, a park since 1872, Muir found little to alarm him in 1898, and his writing is thus descriptive and appreciative of the park's scenic and natural wonders and documentary of its history. Thus it is still a good visitor's guide to the park story.

Muir said he wasn't ever satisfied with his writing until he had read it aloud and it sounded right. Try that yourself and read aloud those passages that appeal to you most. You'll find some almost musical in composition, and will enjoy them—and the world they portray—still more. And that is why Muir lived and wrote: to share the joys he found in the outdoors. You'll see it was not in vain, for this little booklet will help you enjoy Yelowstone, or nature anywhere, still more.   *William R. Jones*, Series Editor

MUD GEYSERS.

IN THE GEYSER BASIN.

The Yellowstone National Park
by John Muir

OF the four national parks of the West, the Yellowstone is far the largest. It is a big, wholesome wilderness on the broad summit of the Rocky Mountains, favored with abundance of rain and snow, — a place of fountains where the greatest of the American rivers take their rise. The central portion is a densely forested and comparatively level volcanic plateau with an average elevation of about eight thousand feet above the sea, surrounded by an imposing host of mountains belonging to the subordinate Gallatin, Wind River, Teton, Absaroka, and snowy ranges. Unnumbered lakes shine in it, united by a famous band of streams that rush up out of hot lava beds, or fall from the frosty peaks in channels rocky and bare, mossy and bosky, to the main rivers, singing cheerily on through every difficulty, cunningly dividing and finding their way east and west to the two far-off seas.

Glacier meadows and beaver meadows are outspread with charming effect along the banks of the streams, parklike expanses in the woods, and innumerable small gardens in rocky recesses of the mountains, some of them containing more petals than leaves, while the whole wilderness is enlivened with happy animals.

Beside the treasures common to most mountain regions that are wild and blessed with a kind climate, the park is full of exciting wonders. The wildest geysers in the world, in bright, triumphant bands, are dancing and singing in it amid thousands of boiling springs, beautiful and awful, their basins arrayed in gorgeous colors like gigantic flowers ; and hot paint-pots, mud springs, mud volcanoes, mush and broth caldrons whose contents are of every color and consistency, plash and heave and roar in bewildering abundance. In the adjacent mountains, beneath the living trees the edges of petrified forests are exposed to view, like specimens on the shelves of a

THE YELLOWSTONE.

museum, standing on ledges tier above tier where they grew, solemnly silent in rigid crystalline beauty after swaying in the winds thousands of centuries ago, opening marvelous views back into the years and climates and life of the past. Here, too, are hills of sparkling crystals, hills of sulphur, hills of glass, hills of cinders and ashes, mountains of every style of architecture, icy or forested, mountains covered with honey-bloom

OBSIDIAN CLIFF, BEAVER LAKE.

sweet as Hymettus, mountains boiled soft like potatoes and colored like a sunset sky. A' that and a' that, and twice as muckle 's a' that, Nature has on show in the Yellowstone Park. Therefore it is called Wonderland, and thousands of tourists and travelers stream into it every summer, and wander about in it enchanted.

Fortunately, almost as soon as it was discovered it was dedicated and set apart for the benefit of the people, a piece of legislation that shines benignly amid the common dust-and-ashes history of the public domain, for which the world must thank Professor Hayden above all others; for he led the first scientific exploring party into it, described it, and with admirable enthusiasm urged Congress to preserve it. As delineated in the year 1872, the park contained about 3344 square miles. On March 30, 1891 it was to all intents and purposes enlarged by the Yellowstone National Park Timber Reserve, and in December, 1897, by the Teton Forest Reserve; thus nearly doubling its original area, and extending the southern boundary far enough to take in the sublime Teton range and the famous pasture-lands of the big Rocky Mountain game animals. The withdrawal of this large tract from the public domain did no harm to any one; for its height, 6000 to over 13,000 feet above the sea, and its thick mantle of volcanic rocks, prevent its ever being available for agriculture or mining, while

on the other hand its geographical position, reviving climate, and wonderful scenery combine
to make it a grand health, pleasure, and study

MINUTE GEYSER, NORRIS GEYSER BASIN.

resort, — a gathering-place for travelers from all the world.

The national parks are not only withdrawn from sale and entry like the forest reservations, but are efficiently managed and guarded by small troops of United States cavalry, directed by the Secretary of the Interior. Under this care the forests are flourishing, protected from both axe and fire ; and so, of course, are the shaggy beds of underbrush and the herbaceous vegetation. The so-called curiosities, also, are preserved, and the furred and feathered tribes, many of which, in danger of extinction a short time ago, are now increasing in numbers, — a refreshing thing to see amid the blind, ruthless destruction that is going on in the adjacent regions. In pleasing contrast to the noisy, ever changing manage-ment, or mismanagement, of blundering, plun-dering, money-making vote-sellers who receive their places from boss politicians as purchased goods, the soldiers do their duty so quietly that the traveler is scarce aware of their presence.

This is the coolest and highest of the parks. Frosts occur every month of the year. Neverthe-less, the tenderest tourist finds it warm enough in summer. The air is electric and full of ozone, healing, reviving, exhilarating, kept pure by frost and fire, while the scenery is wild enough to awaken the dead. It is a glorious place to grow in and rest in ; camping on the shores of the

lakes, in the warm openings of the woods golden
with sunflowers, on the banks of the streams, by
the snowy waterfalls, beside the exciting wonders
or away from them in the scallops of the mountain walls sheltered from every wind, on smooth
silky lawns enameled with gentians, up in the
fountain hollows of the ancient glaciers between
the peaks, where cool pools and brooks and gardens of precious plants charmingly embowered
are never wanting, and good rough rocks with
every variety of cliff and scaur are invitingly
near for outlooks and exercise.

From these lovely dens you may make excursions whenever you like into the middle of the
park, where the geysers and hot springs are reeking and spouting in their beautiful basins, dis-
playing an exuberance of color and strange mo-
tion and energy admirably calculated to surprise
and frighten, charm and shake up the least sensi-
tive out of apathy into newness of life.

However orderly your excursions or aimless,
again and again amid the calmest, stillest scenery
you will be brought to a standstill hushed and
awe-stricken before phenomena wholly new to
you. Boiling springs and huge deep pools of
purest green and azure water, thousands of them,
are plashing and heaving in these high, cool
mountains as if a fierce furnace fire were burning
beneath each one of them; and a hundred geysers, white torrents of boiling water and steam,

THE MUD VOLCANO.

like inverted waterfalls, are ever and anon rushing up out of the hot, black underworld. Some
of these ponderous geyser columns are as large as
sequoias, — five to sixty feet in diameter, one
hundred and fifty to three hundred feet high,
— and are sustained at this great height with
tremendous energy for a few minutes, or perhaps nearly an hour, standing rigid and erect,
hissing, throbbing, booming, as if thunderstorms
were raging beneath their roots, their sides
roughened or fluted like the furrowed boles of
trees, their tops dissolving in feathery branches,
while the irised spray, like misty bloom is at times
blown aside, revealing the massive shafts shining
against a background of pine-covered hills.
Some of them lean more or less, as if storm-bent,
and instead of being round are flat or fan-shaped,
issuing from irregular slits in silex pavements
with radiate structure, the sunbeams sifting
through them in ravishing splendor. Some are
broad and round-headed like oaks; others are
low and bunchy, branching near the ground like
bushes; and a few are hollow in the centre like
big daisies or water-lilies. No frost cools them,
snow never covers them nor lodges in their
branches; winter and summer they welcome alike;
all of them, of whatever form or size, faithfully
rising and sinking in fairy rhythmic dance night
and day, in all sorts of weather, at varying periods
of minutes, hours, or weeks, growing up rapidly,

THE GREAT CANYON AND LOWER FALLS OF THE YELLOWSTONE.

uncontrollable as fate, tossing their pearly
branches in the wind, bursting into bloom and
vanishing like the frailest flowers, — plants of
which Nature raises hundreds or thousands of
crops a year with no apparent exhaustion of the
fiery soil.

The so-called geyser basins, in which this rare
sort of vegetation is growing, are mostly open
valleys on the central plateau that were eroded
by glaciers after the greater volcanic fires had
ceased to burn. Looking down over the forests
as you approach them from the surrounding
heights, you see a multitude of white columns,
broad, reeking masses, and irregular jets and
puffs of misty vapor ascending from the bottom
of the valley, or entangled like smoke among the
neighboring trees, suggesting the factories of
some busy town or the camp-fires of an army.
These mark the position of each mush-pot, paint-
pot, hot spring, and geyser, or gusher, as the
Icelandic words mean. And when you saunter
into the midst of them over the bright sinter
pavements, and see how pure and white and
pearly gray they are in the shade of the mountains, and how radiant in the sunshine, you are
fairly enchanted. So numerous they are and
varied, Nature seems to have gathered them
from all the world as specimens of her rarest
fountains, to show in one place what she can do.
Over four thousand hot springs have been counted

THE GREAT GEYSER BASIN OF THE UPPER YELLOWSTONE.

in the park, and a hundred geysers; how many
more there are nobody knows.

These valleys at the heads of the great rivers
may be regarded as laboratories and kitchens,
in which, amid a thousand retorts and pots, we
may see Nature at work as chemist or cook, cunningly compounding an infinite variety of mineral
messes; cooking whole mountains; boiling and
steaming flinty rocks to smooth paste and mush,
— yellow, brown, red, pink, lavender, gray, and
creamy white, — making the most beautiful mud
in the world; and distilling the most ethereal
essences. Many of these pots and caldrons have
been boiling thousands of years. Pots of sulphurous mush, stringy and lumpy, and pots of
broth as black as ink, are tossed and stirred with
constant care, and thin transparent essences, too
pure and fine to be called water, are kept simmer-
ing gently in beautiful sinter cups and bowls
that grow ever more beautiful the longer they
are used. In some of the spring basins, the
waters, though still warm, are perfectly calm, and
shine blandly in a sod of overleaning grass and
flowers, as if they were thoroughly cooked at last,
and set aside to settle and cool. Others are
wildly boiling over as if running to waste, thousands of tons of the precious liquids being thrown
into the air to fall in scalding floods on the clean
coral floor of the establishment, keeping onlook-
ers at a distance. Instead of holding limpid pale

green or azure water, other pots and craters are filled with scalding mud, which is tossed up from three or four feet to thirty feet, in sticky, rank-smelling masses, with gasping, belching, thudding sounds, plastering the branches of neighboring trees; every flask, retort, hot spring, and geyser has something special in it, no two being the same in temperature, color, or composition.

In these natural laboratories one needs stout faith to feel at ease. The ground sounds hollow underfoot, and the awful subterranean thunder shakes one's mind as the ground is shaken, especially at night in the pale moonlight, or when the sky is overcast with storm-clouds. In the solemn gloom, the geysers, dimly visible, look like monstrous dancing ghosts, and their wild songs and the earthquake thunder replying to the storms overhead seem doubly terrible, as if divine government were at an end. But the trembling hills keep their places. The sky clears, the rosy dawn is reassuring, and up comes the sun like a god, pouring his faithful beams across the mountains and forest, lighting each peak and tree and ghastly geyser alike, and shining into the eyes of the reeking springs, clothing them with rainbow light, and dissolving the seeming chaos of darkness into varied forms of harmony. The ordinary work of the world goes on. Gladly we see the flies dancing in the sun-beams, birds feeding their young, squirrels gath-

MUD SPRINGS.

ering nuts, and hear the blessed ouzel singing confidingly in the shallows of the river, — most faithful evangel, calming every fear, reducing everything to love.

The variously tinted sinter and travertine formations, outspread like pavements over large areas of the geyser valleys, lining the spring basins and throats of the craters, and forming beautiful coral-like rims and curbs about them, always excite admiring attention; so also does the play of the waters from which they are deposited. The various minerals in them are rich in colors, and these are greatly heightened by a smooth, silky growth of brilliantly colored confervæ which lines many of the pools and channels and terraces. No bed of flower-bloom is more exquisite than these myriads of minute plants, visible only in mass, growing in the hot waters. Most of the spring borders are low and daintily scalloped, crenelated, and beaded with sinter pearls. Some of the geyser craters are massive and picturesque, like ruined castles or old burned-out sequoia stumps, and are adorned on a grand scale with outbulging, cauliflower-like formations. From these as centres the silex pavements slope gently away in thin, crusty, overlapping layers, slightly interrupted in some places by low terraces. Or, as in the case of the Mammoth Hot Springs, at the north end of the park, where the building waters issue from the

EXTINCT GEYSER, EAST FORK OF THE YELLOWSTONE.

side of a steep hill, the deposits form a succession
of higher and broader terraces of white travertine tinged with purple, like the famous Pink
Terrace at Rotomahana, New Zealand, draped
in front with clustering stalactites, each terrace
having a pool of indescribably beautiful water
upon it in a basin with a raised rim that glistens
with confervæ, — the whole, when viewed at a
distance of a mile or two, looking like a broad,
massive cascade pouring over shelving rocks in
snowy purpled foam.

The stones of this divine masonry, invisible particles of lime or silex, mined in quarries no eye has seen, go to their appointed places in gentle, tinkling, transparent currents or through the dashing turmoil of floods, as surely guided as the sap of plants streaming into bole and branch, leaf and flower. And thus from century to century this beauty-work has gone on and is going on.

Passing through many a mile of pine and spruce woods, toward the centre of the park you come to the famous Yellowstone Lake. It is about twenty miles long and fifteen wide, and lies at a height of nearly 8000 feet above the level of the sea, amid dense black forests and snowy mountains. Around its winding, wavering shores, closely forested and picturesquely varied with promontories and bays, the distance is more than 100 miles. It is not very deep,

YELLOWSTONE LAKE.

only from 200 to 300 feet, and contains less water than the celebrated Lake Tahoe of the California Sierra, which is nearly the same size, lies at a height of 6400 feet, and is over 1600 feet deep. But no other lake in North America of equal area lies so high as the Yellowstone, or gives birth to so noble a river. The terraces around its shores show that at the close of the glacial period its surface was about 160 feet higher than it is now, and its area nearly twice as great.

It is full of trout, and a vast multitude of birds — swans, pelicans, geese, ducks, cranes, herons, curlews, plovers, snipe — feed in it and upon its shores; and many forest animals come out of the woods, and wade a little way in shallow, sandy places to drink and look about them, and cool themselves in the free flowing breezes.

In calm weather it is a magnificent mirror for the woods and mountains and sky, now pattered with hail and rain, now roughened with sudden storms that send waves to fringe the shores and wash its border of gravel and sand. The Absaroka Mountains and the Wind River Plateau on the east and south pour their gathered waters into it, and the river issues from the north side in a broad, smooth, stately current, silently gliding with such serene majesty that one fancies it knows the vast journey of four thousand miles that lies before it, and the work it has to do.

For the first twenty miles its course is in a level,
sunny valley lightly fringed with trees, through
which it flows in silvery reaches stirred into
spangles here and there by ducks and leaping
trout, making no sound save a low whispering
among the pebbles and the dipping willows and
sedges of its banks. Then suddenly, as if pre-
paring for hard work, it rushes eagerly, impetu-
ously forward rejoicing in its strength, breaks
into foam-bloom, and goes thundering down into
the Grand Cañon in two magnificent falls, one
hundred and three hundred feet high.

The cañon is so tremendously wild and impressive that even these great falls cannot hold
your attention. It is about twenty miles long
and a thousand feet deep, — a weird, unearthly-
looking gorge of jagged, fantastic architecture,
and most brilliantly colored. Here the Washburn range, forming the northern rim of the
Yellowstone basin, made up mostly of beds of
rhyolite decomposed by the action of thermal
waters, has been cut through and laid open to
view by the river; and a famous section it has
made. It is not the depth or the shape of the
cañon, nor the waterfall, nor the green and gray
river chanting its brave song as it goes foaming
on its way, that most impresses the observer, but
the colors of the decomposed volcanic rocks.
With few exceptions, the traveler in strange
lands finds that, however much the scenery and

GREAT CAÑON OF THE YELLOWSTONE.

vegetation in different countries may change, Mother Earth is ever familiar and the same. But here the very ground is changed, as if belonging to some other world. The walls of the cañon from top to bottom burn in a perfect glory of color, confounding and dazzling when the sun is shining, — white, yellow, green, blue, vermilion, and various other shades of red indefinitely blending. All the earth hereabouts seems to be paint. Millions of tons of it lie in sight, exposed to wind and weather as if of no account, yet marvelously fresh and bright, fast colors not to be washed out or bleached out by either sunshine or storms. The effect is so novel and awful, we imagine that even a river might be afraid to enter such a place. But the rich and gentle beauty of the vegetation is reassuring. The lovely Linnæa borealis hangs her twin bells over the brink of the cliffs, forests and gardens extend their treasures in smiling confidence on either side, nuts and berries ripen well whatever may be going on below; blind fears vanish, and the grand gorge seems a kindly, beautiful part of the general harmony, full of peace and joy and good will.

The park is easy of access. Locomotives drag you to its northern boundary at Cinnabar, and horses and guides do the rest. From Cinnabar you will be whirled in coaches along the foaming Gardiner River to Mammoth Hot Springs;

WHITE MOUNTAIN, MAMMOTH SPRINGS.

thence through woods and meadows, gulches and ravines along branches of the Upper Gallatin, Madison, and Firehole rivers to the main geyser basins; thence over the Continental Divide and back again, up and down through dense pine, spruce, and fir woods to the magnificent Yellowstone Lake, along its northern shore to the outlet, down the river to the falls and Grand Cañon, and thence back through the woods to Mammoth Hot Springs and Cinnabar; stopping here and there at the so-called points of interest among

the geysers, springs, paint-pots, mud volcanoes,
etc., where you will be allowed a few minutes or
hours to saunter over the sinter pavements,
watch the play of a few of the geysers, and peer
into some of the most beautiful and terrible of
the craters and pools. These wonders you will
enjoy, and also the views of the mountains, especially the Gallatin and Absaroka ranges, the
long, willowy glacier and beaver meadows, the
beds of violets, gentians, phloxes, asters, phace-
lias, goldenrods, eriogonums, and many other
flowers, some species giving color to whole
meadows and hillsides. And you will enjoy
your short views of the great lake and river and

CASTLE GEYSER AND FIRE BASIN.

cañon. No scalping Indians will you see. The
Blackfeet and Bannocks that once roamed here
are gone; so are the old beaver-catchers, the
Coulters and Bridgers, with all their attractive
buckskin and romance. There are several bands

GOLDEN GATE AND BRIDGE.

of buffaloes in the park, but you will not thus cheaply in tourist fashion see them nor many of the other large animals hidden in the wilderness. The song-birds, too, keep mostly out of sight of the rushing tourist, though off the roads thrushes, warblers, orioles, grosbeaks, etc., keep the air sweet and merry. Perhaps in passing rapids and falls you may catch glimpses of the water-ouzel, but in the whirling noise you will not hear his song. Fortunately, no road noise frightens the Douglas squirrel, and his merry play and gossip will amuse you all through the woods. Here and there a deer may be seen crossing the road, or a bear. Most likely, however, the only bears you will see are the half tame ones that go to the hotels every night for dinner-table scraps, — yeast-powder biscuit, Chicago canned stuff, mixed pickles, and beefsteaks that have proved too tough for the tourists.

Among the gains of a coach trip are the acquaintances made and the fresh views into human nature ; for the wilderness is a shrewd touchstone, even thus lightly approached, and brings many a curious trait to view. Setting out, the driver cracks his whip, and the four horses go off at half gallop, half trot, in trained, showy style, until out of sight of the hotel. The coach is crowded, old and young side by side, blooming and fading, full of hope and fun and care. Some look at the scenery or the horses,

THE GIANT GEYSER.

and all ask questions, an odd mixed lot of them:
"Where is the umbrella? What is the name of
that blue flower over there? Are you sure the
little bag is aboard? Is that hollow yonder a
crater? How is your throat this morning?
How high did you say the geysers spout? How
does the elevation affect your head? Is that a
geyser reeking over there in the rocks, or only a
hot spring?" A long ascent is made, the solemn
mountains come to view, small cares are quenched,
and all become natural and silent, save perhaps
some unfortunate expounder who has been read-
ing guidebook geology, and rumbles forth foggy
subsidences and upheavals until he is in danger
of being heaved overboard. The driver will

give you the names of the peaks and meadows
and streams as you come to them, call attention
to the glass road, tell how hard it was to build,
— how the obsidian cliffs naturally pushed the
surveyor's lines to the right, and the industrious
beavers, by flooding the valley in front of the
cliff, pushed them to the left.

Geysers, however, are the main objects, and as
soon as they come in sight other wonders are forgotten. All gather around the crater of the one
that is expected to play first. During the erup-
tions of the smaller geysers, such as the Beehive
and Old Faithful, though a little frightened at
first, all welcome the glorious show with enthusiasm, and shout, " Oh, how wonderful, beautiful,
splendid, majestic ! " Some venture near enough
to stroke the column with a stick, as if it were
a stone pillar or a tree, so firm and substantial
and permanent it seems. While tourists wait
around a large geyser, such as the Castle or the
Giant, there is a chatter of small talk in anything
but solemn mood; and during the intervals
between the preliminary splashes and upheavals
some adventurer occasionally looks down the
throat of the crater, admiring the silex formations and wondering whether Hades is as beautiful. But when, with awful uproar as if avalanches were falling and storms thundering in
the depths, the tremendous outburst begins,
all run away to a safe distance, and look on,

THE GRAND CANYON.

awe-stricken and silent, in devout, worshiping wonder.

The largest and one of the most wonderfully beautiful of the springs is the Prismatic, which the guide will be sure to show you. With a circumference of 300 yards, it is more like a lake than a spring. The water is pure deep blue in the centre, fading to green on the edges, and its basin and the slightly terraced pavement about it are astonishingly bright and varied in color. This one of the multitude of Yellowstone fountains is of itself object enough for a trip across the continent. No wonder that so many fine myths have originated in springs; that so many fountains were held sacred in the youth of the world, and had miraculous virtues ascribed to them. Even in these cold, doubting, questioning, scientific times many of the Yellowstone fountains seem able to work miracles. Near the Prismatic Spring is the great Excelsior Geyser, which is said to throw a column of boiling water 60 to 70 feet in diameter to a height of from 50 to 300 feet, at irregular periods. This is the greatest of all the geysers yet discovered anywhere. The Firehole River, which sweeps past it, is, at ordinary stages, a stream about 100 yards wide and 3 feet deep; but when the geyser is in eruption, so great is the quantity of water discharged that the volume of the river is doubled, and it is rendered too hot and rapid to be forded.

Geysers are found in many other volcanic regions, — in Iceland, New Zealand, Japan, the Himalayas, the Eastern Archipelago, South America, the Azores, and elsewhere; but only in Iceland, New Zealand, and this Rocky Mountain park do they display their grandest forms, and of these three famous regions the Yellowstone is easily first, both in the number and in the size of its geysers. The greatest height of the column of the Great Geyser of Iceland actually measured was 212 feet, and of the Strokhr 162 feet.

In New Zealand, the Te Pueia at Lake Taupo, the Waikite at Rotorna, and two others are said to lift their waters occasionally to a height of 100 feet, while the celebrated Te Tarata at Rotomahana

MAMMOTH HOT SPRINGS HOTEL, YELLOWSTONE NATIONAL PARK.
(*Reached by Northern Pacific Railroad.*)

sometimes lifts a boiling column 20 feet in diameter to a height of 60 feet. But all these are far surpassed by the Excelsior. Few tourists, however, will see the Excelsior in action, or a thousand other interesting features of the park that lie beyond the wagon-roads and the hotels. The regular trips — from three to five days — are too short. Nothing can be done well at a speed of forty miles a day. The multitude of mixed, novel impressions rapidly piled on one another make only a dreamy, bewildering, swirling blur, most of which is unrememberable. Far more time should be taken. Walk away quietly in any direction and taste the freedom of the mountaineer. Camp out among the grass and gentians of glacier meadows, in craggy garden nooks full of Nature's darlings. Climb the mountains and get their good tidings. Nature's peace will flow into you as sunshine flows into trees. The winds will blow their own freshness into you, and the storms their energy, while cares will drop off like autumn leaves. As age comes on, one source of enjoyment after another is closed, but Nature's sources never fail. Like a generous host, she offers here brimming cups in endless variety, served in a grand hall, the sky its ceiling, the mountains its walls, decorated with glorious paintings and enlivened with bands of music ever playing. The petty discomforts that beset the awkward guest, the unskilled camper, are quickly

The Old Faithful Geyser

Bee Hive Castle Geyser

The Giant Geyser

forgotten, while all that is precious remains. Fears vanish as soon as one is fairly free in the wilderness.

Most of the dangers that haunt the unseasoned citizen are imaginary; the real ones are perhaps too few rather than too many for his good. The bears that always seem to spring up thick as trees, in fighting, devouring attitudes before the frightened tourist whenever a camping trip is proposed, are gentle now, finding they are no longer likely to be shot; and rattlesnakes, the other big irrational dread of over-civilized people, are scarce here, for most of the park lies above the snake-line. Poor creatures, loved only by their Maker, they are timid and bashful, as mountaineers know; and though perhaps not possessed of much of that charity that suffers long and is kind, seldom, either by mistake or by mishap, do harm to any one. Certainly they cause not the hundredth part of the pain and death that follow the footsteps of the admired Rocky Mountain trapper. Nevertheless, again and again, in season and out of season, the question comes up, "What are rattlesnakes good for?" As if nothing that does not obviously make for the benefit of man had any right to exist; as if our ways were God's ways. Long ago, an Indian to whom a French traveler put this old question replied that their tails were good for toothache, and their heads for fever.

Anyhow, they are all, head and tail, good for themselves, and we need not begrudge them their share of life.

Fear nothing. No town park you have been accustomed to saunter in is so free from danger as the Yellowstone. It is a hard place to leave. Even its names in your guidebook are attractive, and should draw you far from wagon-roads, — all save the early ones, derived from the infernal regions: Hell Roaring River, Hell Broth Springs, The Devil's Caldron, etc. Indeed, the whole region was at first called Coulter's Hell, from the fiery brimstone stories told by trapper Coulter, who left the Lewis and Clark expedition and wandered through the park, in the year 1807, with a band of Bannock Indians. The later names, many of which we owe to Mr. Arnold Hague of the U. S. Geological Survey, are so telling and exhilarating that they set our pulses dancing and make us begin to enjoy the pleasures of excursions ere they are commenced. Three River Peak, Two Ocean Pass, Continental Divide, are capital geographical descriptions, suggesting thousands of miles of rejoicing streams and all that belongs to them. Big Horn Pass, Bison Peak, Big Game Ridge, bring brave mountain animals to mind. Birch Hills, Garnet Hills, Amethyst Mountain, Storm Peak, Electric Peak, Roaring Mountain, are bright, bracing names. Wapiti, Beaver, Tern, and Swan lakes, conjure

CLIFFS ON THE YELLOWSTONE.

up fine pictures, and so also do Osprey and Ouzel falls. Antelope Creek, Otter, Mink, and Grayling creeks, Geode, Jasper, Opal, Carnelian, and Chalcedony creeks, are lively and sparkling names that help the streams to shine; and Azalea, Stellaria, Arnica, Aster, and Phlox creeks, what pictures these bring up! Violet, Morning Mist, Hygeia, Beryl, Vermilion, and Indigo springs, and many beside, give us visions of fountains more beautifully arrayed than Solomon in all his purple and golden glory. All these and a host of others call you to camp. You may be a little cold some nights, on mountain tops above the timber-line, but you will see the stars, and by and by you can sleep enough in your town bed, or at least in your grave. Keep awake while you may in mountain mansions so rare.

If you are not very strong, try to climb Electric Peak when a big bossy, well-charged thunder-cloud is on it, to breathe the ozone set free, and get yourself kindly shaken and shocked. You are sure to be lost in wonder and praise, and every hair of your head will stand up and hum and sing like an enthusiastic congregation.

After this reviving experience, you should take a look into a few of the tertiary volumes of the grand geological library of the park, and see how God writes history. No technical knowledge is required; only a calm day and a calm mind. Perhaps nowhere else in the Rocky Mountains have

the volcanic forces been so busy. More than
ten thousand square miles hereabouts have been
covered to a depth of at least five thousand feet
with material spouted from chasms and craters
during the tertiary period, forming broad sheets
of basalt, andesite, rhyolite, etc., and marvelous
masses of ashes, sand, cinders, and stones now
consolidated into conglomerates, charged with the
remains of plants and animals that lived in the
calm, genial periods that separated the volcanic
outbursts.

Perhaps the most interesting and telling of
these rocks, to the hasty tourist, are those that
make up the mass of Amethyst Mountain. On its
north side it presents a section two thousand feet
high of roughly stratified beds of sand, ashes, and
conglomerates coarse and fine, forming the un-
trimmed edges of a wonderful set of volumes ly-
ing on their sides, — books a million years old,
well bound, miles in size, with full-page illustrations. On the ledges of this one section we see
trunks and stumps of fifteen or twenty ancient
forests ranged one above another, standing where
they grew, or prostrate and broken like the pil-
lars of ruined temples in desert sands, — a forest
fifteen or twenty stories high, the roots of each
spread above the tops of the next beneath it, telling wonderful tales of the bygone centuries, with
their winters and summers, growth and death,
fire, ice, and flood.

There were giants in those days. The largest
of the standing opal and agate stumps and prostrate sections of the trunks are from two or three
to fifty feet in height or length, and from five
to ten feet in diameter ; and so perfect is the pet-
rifaction that the annual rings and ducts are
clearer and more easily counted than those of
living trees, centuries of burial having brightened
the records instead of blurring them. They show
that the winters of the tertiary period gave as
decided a check to vegetable growth as do those
of the present time. Some trees favorably lo-
cated grew rapidly, increasing twenty inches in
diameter in as many years, while others of the
same species, on poorer soil or overshadowed, in-

PETRIFIED TREES.

THE BEE-HIVE.

creased only two or three inches in the same time.

Among the roots and stumps on the old forest floors we find the remains of ferns and bushes, and the seeds and leaves of trees like those now growing on the southern Alleghanies, — such as magnolia, sassafras, laurel, linden, persimmon, ash, alder, dogwood. Studying the lowest of these forests, the soil it grew on and the deposits it is buried in, we see that it was rich in species, and flourished in a genial, sunny climate. When its stately trees were in their glory, volcanic fires broke forth from chasms and craters, like larger geysers, spouting ashes, cinders, stones, and mud, which fell on the doomed forest like hail and

snow; sifting, hurtling through the leaves and
branches, choking the streams, covering the
ground, crushing bushes and ferns, rapidly deep-
ening, packing around +he trees and breaking
them, rising higher until the topmost boughs of
the giants were buried, leaving not a leaf or twig
in sight, so complete was the desolation. At last
the volcanic storm began to abate, the fiery soil
settled; mud floods and boulder floods passed
over it, enriching it, cooling it; rains fell and
mellow sunshine, and it became fertile and ready
for another crop. Birds, and the winds, and
roaming animals brought seeds from more fortu-
nate woods, and a new forest grew up on the top
of the buried one. Centuries of genial growing
seasons passed. The seedling trees became giants,
and with strong outreaching branches spread a
leafy canopy over the gray land.

The sleeping subterranean fires again awake
and shake the mountains, and every leaf trem-
bles. The old craters, with perhaps new ones, are
opened, and immense quantities of ashes, pumice,
and cinders are again thrown into the sky. The
sun, shorn of his beams, glows like a dull red
ball, until hidden in sulphurous clouds. Volcanic
snow, hail, and floods fall on the new forest,
burying it alive, like the one beneath its roots.
Then come another noisy band of mud floods
and boulder floods, mixing, settling, enriching
the new ground, more seeds, quickening sun-

"THE GIANTESS."

shine and showers; and a third noble magnolia
forest is carefully raised on the top of the second.
And so on. Forest was planted above forest
and destroyed, as if Nature were ever repenting,
undoing the work she had so industriously done,
and burying it.

Of course this destruction was creation, pro-
gress in the march of beauty through death.
How quickly these old monuments excite and
hold the imagination! We see the old stone
stumps budding and blossoming and waving in
the wind as magnificent trees, standing shoulder
to shoulder, branches interlacing in grand varied
round-headed forests; see the sunshine of morning and evening gilding their mossy trunks, and
at high noon spangling on the thick glossy
leaves of the magnolia, filtering through translu-
cent canopies of linden and ash, and falling in
mellow patches on the ferny floor; see the shining after rain, breathe the exhaling fragrance,
and hear the winds and birds and the murmur
of brooks and insects. We watch them from season to season; see the swelling buds when the
sap begins to flow in the spring, the opening
leaves and blossoms, the ripening of summer
fruits, the colors of autumn, and the maze of
leafless branches and sprays in winter; and we
see the sudden oncome of the storms that over-
whelmed them.

One calm morning at sunrise I saw the oaks

THE HOT SPRINGS NEAR GARDINER'S RIVER.

and pines in Yosemite Valley shaken by an earthquake, their tops swishing back and forth, and
every branch and needle shuddering as if in dis-
tress like the frightened screaming birds. One
may imagine the trembling, rocking, tumultuous
waving of those ancient Yellowstone woods, and
the terror of their inhabitants when the first
foreboding shocks were felt, the sky grew dark,
and rock-laden floods began to roar. But though
they were close pressed and buried, cut off from
sun and wind, all their happy leaf-fluttering and
waving done, other currents coursed through
them, fondling and thrilling every fibre, and
beautiful wood was replaced by beautiful stone.
Now their rocky sepulchres are partly open, and
show forth the natural beauty of death.

After the forest times and fire times had
passed away, and the volcanic furnaces were
banked and held in abeyance, another great
change occurred. The glacial winter came on.
The sky was again darkened, not with dust and
ashes, but with snow which fell in glorious abundance, piling deeper, deeper, slipping from the
overladen heights in booming avalanches, com-
pacting into glaciers, that flowed over all the
landscape, wiping off forests, grinding, sculptur-
ing, fashioning the comparatively featureless
lava beds into the beautiful rhythm of hill and
dale and ranges of mountains we behold to-day ;
forming basins for lakes, channels for streams,

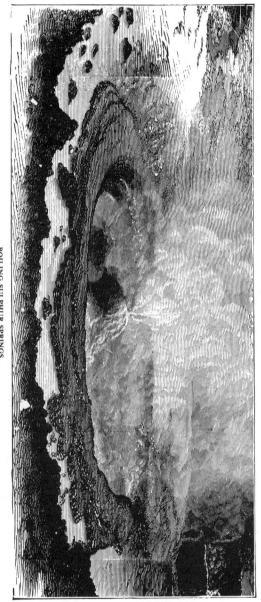

BOILING SULPHUR SPRINGS.

new soils for forests, gardens, and meadows.
While this ice-work was going on, the slumber-
ing volcanic fires were boiling the subterranean
waters, and with curious chemistry decomposing
the rocks, making beauty in the darkness; these
forces, seemingly antagonistic, working harmo-
niously together. How wild their meetings on
the surface were we may imagine. When the
glacier period began, geysers and hot springs
were playing in grander volume, it may be, than
those of to-day. The glaciers flowed over them
while they spouted and thundered, carrying away
their fine sinter and travertine structures, and
shortening their mysterious channels.

The soils made in the down-grinding required
to bring the present features of the landscape
into relief are possibly no better than were some
of the old volcanic soils that were carried away,
and which, as we have seen, nourished magnificent forests, but the glacial landscapes are incom-
parably more beautiful than the old volcanic
ones were. The glacial winter has passed away,
like the ancient summers and fire periods, though
in the chronolgy of the geologist all these times
are recent. Only small residual glaciers on the
cool northern slopes of the highest mountains
are left of the vast all-embracing ice-mantle, as
solfataras and geysers are all that are left of the
ancient volcanoes.

Now the post-glacial agents are at work on the

grand old palimpsest of the park region, inscribing new characters; but still in its main telling features it remains distinctly glacial. The moraine soils are being leveled, sorted, refined, re-formed, and covered with vegetation; the polished pavements and scoring and other superficial glacial inscriptions on the crumbling lavas are being rapidly obliterated; gorges are being cut in the decomposed rhyolites and loose conglomerates, and turrets and pinnacles seem to be springing up like growing trees; while the geysers are depositing miles of sinter and travertine. Nevertheless, the ice-work is scarce blurred as yet. These later effects are only spots and wrinkles on the grand glacial countenance of the park.

Perhaps you have already said that you have seen enough for a lifetime. But before you go away you should spend at least one day and a night on a mountain top, for a last general, calming, settling view. Mount Washburn is a good one for the purpose, because it stands in the middle of the park, is unencumbered with other peaks, and is so easy of access that the climb to its summit is only a saunter. First your eye goes roving around the mountain rim amid the hundreds of peaks : some with plain flowing skirts, others abruptly precipitous and defended by sheer battlemented escarpments; flat-topped or round; heaving like sea-waves or spired and

UPPER FALLS OF THE YELLOWSTONE.

turreted like Gothic cathedrals; streaked with snow in the ravines, and darkened with files of adventurous trees climbing the ridges. The nearer peaks are perchance clad in sapphire blue, others far off in creamy white. In the broad glare of noon they seem to shrink and crouch to less than half their real stature, and grow dull and uncommunicative, — mere dead, draggled heaps of waste ashes and stone, giving no hint of the multitude of animals enjoying life in their fastnesses, or of the bright bloom-bordered streams and lakes. But when storms blow they awake and arise, wearing robes of cloud and mist in majestic speaking attitudes like gods. In the color glory of morning and evening they become still more impressive ; steeped in the divine light of the alpenglow their earthiness disappears, and, blending with the heavens, they seem neither high nor low.

Over all the central plateau, which from here seems level, and over the foothills and lower slopes of the mountains, the forest extends like a black uniform bed of weeds, interrupted only by lakes and meadows and small burned spots called parks, — all of them, except the Yellowstone Lake, being mere dots and spangles in general views, made conspicuous by their color and brightness. About eighty-five per cent of the entire area of the park is covered with trees, mostly the indomitable lodge-pole pine (*Pinus*

contorta, var. *Murrayana*), with a few patches
and sprinklings of Douglas spruce, Engelmann
spruce, silver fir (*Abies lasiocarpa*), Pinus flexilis, and a few alders, aspens, and birches. The
Douglas spruce is found only on the lowest por-
tions, the silver fir on the highest, and the Engelmann spruce on the dampest places, best defended
from fire. Some fine specimens of the flexilis
pine are growing on the margins of openings, —
wide-branching, sturdy trees, as broad as high,
with trunks five feet in diameter, leafy and
shady, laden with purple cones and rose-colored
flowers. The Engelmann spruce and sub-alpine
silver fir are beautiful and notable trees, —
tall, spiry, hardy, frost and snow defying, and
widely distributed over the West, wherever there
is a mountain to climb or a cold moraine slope
to cover. But neither of these is a good fire-
fighter. With rather thin bark, and scattering
their seeds every year as soon as they are ripe,
they are quickly driven out of fire-swept regions. When the glaciers were melting, these
hardy mountaineering trees were probably among
the first to arrive on the new moraine soil beds;
but as the plateau became drier and fires began
to run, they were driven up the mountains, and
into the wet spots and islands where we now find
them, leaving nearly all the park to the lodge-
pole pine, which, though as thin-skinned as they
and as easily killed by fire, takes pains to store

up its seeds in firmly closed cones, and holds them from three to nine years, so that, let the fire come when it may, it is ready to die and ready to live again in a new generation. For when the killing fires have devoured the leaves and thin resinous bark, many of the cones, only scorched, open as soon as the smoke clears away; the hoarded store of seeds is sown broadcast on the cleared ground, and a new growth immediately springs up triumphant out of the ashes. Therefore, this tree not only holds its ground, but extends its conquests farther after every fire. Thus the evenness and closeness of its growth are accounted for. In one part of the forest that I examined, the growth was about as close as a cane-brake. The trees were from four to eight inches in diameter, one hundred feet high, and one hundred and seventy-five years old. The lower limbs die young and drop off for want of light. Life with these close-planted trees is a race for light, more light, and so they push straight for the sky. Mowing off ten feet from the top of the forest would make it look like a crowded mass of tele-graph-poles; for only the sunny tops are leafy. A sapling ten years old, growing in the sunshine, has as many leaves as a crowded tree one or two hundred years old. As fires are multiplied and the mountains become drier, this wonderful lodge-pole pine bids fair to obtain possession of nearly all the forest ground in the West.

TOWER FALLS.

How still the woods seem from here, yet how lively a stir the hidden animals are making; digging, gnawing, biting, eyes shining, at work and play, getting food, rearing young, roving through the underbrush, climbing the rocks, wading solitary marshes, tracing the banks of the lakes and streams! Insect swarms are dancing in the sunbeams, burrowing in the ground, diving, swimming,—a cloud of witnesses telling Nature's joy. The plants are as busy as the animals, every cell in a swirl of enjoyment, humming like a hive, singing the old new song of creation. A few columns and puffs of steam are seen rising above the treetops, some near, but most of them far off, indicating geysers and hot springs, gentle-looking and noiseless as downy clouds, softly hinting the reaction going on between the surface and the hot interior. From here you see them better than when you are standing beside them, frightened and confused, regarding them as lawless cataclysms. The shocks and outbursts of earthquakes, volcanoes, geysers, storms, the pounding of waves, the uprush of sap in plants, each and all tell the orderly love-beats of Nature's heart.

Turning to the eastward, you have the Grand Cañon and reaches of the river in full view; and yonder to the southward lies the great lake, the largest and most important of all the high fountains of the Missouri-Mississippi, and the last to be discovered.

In the year 1541, when De Soto, with a romantic band of adventurers, was seeking gold and glory and the fountain of youth, he found the Mississippi a few hundred miles above its mouth, and made his grave beneath its floods. La Salle, in 1682, after discovering the Ohio, one of the largest and most beautiful branches of the Mississippi, traced the latter to the sea from the mouth of the Illinois, through adventures and privations not easily realized now. About the same time Joliet and Father Marquette reached the " Father of Waters " by way of the Wisconsin, but more than a century passed ere its highest sources in these mountains were seen. The advancing stream of civilization has ever followed its guidance toward the west, but none of the thousand tribes of Indians living on its banks could tell the explorer whence it came. From those romantic De Soto and La Salle days to these times of locomotives and tourists, how much has the great river seen and done! Great as it now is, and still growing longer through the ground of its delta and the basins of receding glaciers at its head, it was immensely broader toward the close of the glacial period, when the ice-mantle of the mountains was melting : then with its three hundred thousand miles of branches outspread over the plains and valleys of the continent, laden with fertile mud, it made the biggest and most generous bed of soil in the world.

CRYSTAL FALLS.

Think of this mighty stream springing in the first place in vapor from the sea, flying on the wind, alighting on the mountains in hail and snow and rain, lingering in many a fountain feeding the trees and grass; then gathering its scattered waters, gliding from its noble lake, and going back home to the sea, singing all the way! On it sweeps, through the gates of the mountains, across the vast prairies and plains, through many a wild, gloomy forest, cane-brake, and sunny savanna; from glaciers and snowbanks and pine woods to warm groves of magnolia and palm; geysers dancing at its head keeping time with the sea-waves at its mouth; roaring and gray in rapids, booming in broad, bossy falls, murmuring, gleaming in long, silvery reaches, swaying now hither, now thither, whirling, bending in huge doubling, eddying folds, serene, majestic, ungovernable, overflowing all its metes and bounds, frightening the dwellers upon its banks; building, wasting, uprooting, planting; engulfing old islands and making new ones, taking away fields and towns as if in sport, carrying canoes and ships of commerce in the midst of its spoils and drift, fertilizing the continent as one vast farm. Then, its work done, it gladly vanishes in its ocean home, welcomed by the waiting waves.

Thus naturally, standing here in the midst of its fountains, we trace the fortunes of the great river. And how much more comes to mind as

LOWER FALLS, YELLOWSTONE.

we overlook this wonderful wilderness! Fountains of the Columbia and Colorado lie before
us, interlaced with those of the Yellowstone and
Missouri, and fine it would be to go with them to
the Pacific; but the sun is already in the west,
and soon our day will be done.

Yonder is Amethyst Mountain, and other
mountains hardly less rich in old forests, which
now seem to spring up again in their glory; and
you see the storms that buried them, — the ashes
and torrents laden with boulders and mud, the
centuries of sunshine, and the dark, lurid nights.
You see again the vast floods of lava, red-hot and
white-hot, pouring out from gigantic geysers,
usurping the basins of lakes and streams, absorb-
ing or driving away their hissing, screaming
waters, flowing around hills and ridges, submerg-
ing every subordinate feature. Then you see
the snow and glaciers taking possession of the
land, making new landscapes. How admirable
it is that, after passing through so many vicissi-
tudes of frost and fire and flood, the physiog-
nomy and even the complexion of the landscape
should still be so divinely fine!

Thus reviewing the eventful past, we see Nature working with enthusiasm like a man, blowing
her volcanic forges like a blacksmith blowing
his smithy fires, shoving glaciers over the landscapes like a carpenter shoving his planes, clear-
ing, ploughing, harrowing, irrigating, planting,

and sowing broadcast like a farmer and gardener, doing rough work and fine work, planting sequoias and pines, rosebushes and daisies; working in gems, filling every crack and hollow with them; distilling fine essences; painting plants and shells, clouds, mountains, all the earth and heavens, like an artist, — ever working toward beauty higher and higher. Where may the mind find more stimulating, quickening pasturage? A thousand Yellowstone wonders are calling, " Look up and down and round about you ! " And a multitude of still, small voices may be heard directing you to look through all this transient, shifting show of things called " substantial " into the truly substantial, spiritual world whose forms flesh and wood, rock and water, air and sunshine, only veil and conceal, and to learn that here is heaven and the dwelling-place of the angels.

The sun is setting; long, violet shadows are growing out over the woods from the mountains along the western rim of the park; the Absaroka range is baptized in the divine light of the alpenglow, and its rocks and trees are transfigured. Next to the light of the dawn on high mountain tops, the alpenglow is the most impressive of all the terrestrial manifestations of God.

Now comes the gloaming. The alpenglow is fading into earthy, murky gloom, but do not let your town habits draw you away to the hotel.

Stay on this good fire-mountain and spend the
night among the stars. Watch their glorious
bloom until the dawn, and get one more baptism
of light. Then, with fresh heart, go down to
your work, and whatever your fate, under whatever ignorance or knowledge you may afterward
chance to suffer, you will remember these fine,
wild views, and look back with joy to your wan-
derings in the blessed old Yellowstone Wonderland.

THE LOWER CANYON.